FAST TRACK

PHONICS

For Young Adults and Adults

Kaye Wiley

Longman

The International Phonetic Alphabet

Consonants

/b/	baby, tub
/d/	down, today, sad
/f/	fun, off, phone, elephant
/g/	girl, big
/h/	home, behind
/k/	key, black, picnic
/l/	like, pail
/m/	mat, summer, swim
/n/	no, winter, pan
/ŋ/	sing
/p/	pot, purple, map
/r/	rain, around, door, write
/s/	sister, bus
/š/	she, fish
/t/	tent, little
/θ/	think, math
/ð/	this, clothes, brother
/v/	van, have, of
/w/	wave, one
/y/	yes
/z/	quiz, nose
/ž/	measure
/č/	check, watch
/ǰ/	job, cage

Vowels

/ɑ/	on, hot, father
/æ/	hat, back
/ɛ/	egg, pen, says, head
/ɪ/	in, hill
/ɔ/	off, lot, cannot
/e/	make, train, say
/i/	see, read, key, field
/o/	open, rose, boat, slow
/ü/	flute, boot, do, you, fruit
/ʌ/	up, bus, of
/u/	put
/ə/	the, around
/ɚ/	mother, doctor
/ɝ/	her, bird, nurse

Diphthongs

/ɑɪ/	like, my, pie, night
/ɑu/	out, down, how
/ɔɪ/	noise, boy

The English Alphabet

Here is the pronunciation of the letters of the English alphabet, written in International Phonetic Alphabet symbols.

a	/e/	j	/ǰe/	s	/ɛs/		
b	/bi/	k	/ke/	t	/ti/		
c	/si/	l	/ɛl/	u	/yu/		
d	/di/	m	/ɛm/	v	/vi/		
e	/i/	n	/ɛn/	w	/'dʌbəlˌyu/		
f	/ɛf/	o	/o/	x	/ɛks/		
g	/ǰi/	p	/pi/	y	/wɑɪ/		
h	/eč/	q	/kyu/	z	/zi/		
i	/ɑɪ/	r	/ɑr/				

Preface

Fast Track Phonics is a highly visual program of phonics activities written especially for older English language learners. Each unit contains carefully controlled, high-frequency words embedded in the context of simple, decodable sentences. Clear illustrations enhance comprehension and give new readers a rapid sense of success.

Fast Track Phonics features the activities, games, and outings of the Phonics Team. All the characters of this Team—Pat, Tom, Will, Jen, May, Mike, Steve, and Luz—have short names chosen to highlight English vowel sounds. Since many languages share common consonant sounds with English, the first units of *Fast Track Phonics* do not review initial consonants, but begin instead with contrastive vowel sounds.

Fast Track Phonics activities progress from one-syllable, short-vowel words (*Pat has a van*) to long-vowel words (*Mike rides a bike*) to longer syntax with more complex sound–symbol relationships, like consonant blends and digraphs (*Math problems make you think*). At the top of each page, new sounds and spellings are highlighted in red. Irregular pronunciations are indicated by an icon ⚷ that refers students to the list of Irregular Words at the back of the book. At the end of each unit, the Phonics Team characters provide the backdrop for humorous photo stories and short plays, which students can read, act out, and role-play. These stories are designed to reinforce previously introduced vocabulary and are full of fun and surprises.

Fast Track Phonics also includes two other teaching strands besides phonics: (1) grammar topics and (2) ELD themes (see chart of units 1–5 below). A complete Scope and Sequence chart, along with detailed lesson plans and supplementary activities, is available in the *Fast Track Phonics Teacher's Guide*.

Phonic Element	Sample Grammar Topics	Sample ELD Themes
Unit 1: short vowels: *a, o, i*	verbs: *has, can, sit, is, jog* prepositions: *on, off, in* negative forms: *is not, cannot* possessive form: *…'s*	transportation, sports, animals, household objects
Unit 2: short vowels: *u, e*	verbs: *run, get* yes/no question forms plural forms: adding *s, es*	recreation, weather, numbers, parts of the body, colors
Unit 3: blends (*cl, tr, st, tr, sw*, etc.)	verbs: *spill, smell, swim, jump* preposition: *next to*	classroom objects, animals, vehicles, jobs
Unit 4: long vowels: *a*	verbs: *make, take, wait, play* contractions: *can't, isn't* exclamations: *Great! Hey!*	outdoor activities, food, time, weather, emotions, nature
Unit 5: long vowels: *i*	verbs: *drive, ride, like, cry* personal pronouns: *I, my* adjectives: *wide, fast, five*	recreation, numbers, likes/dislikes, clocks/time, parts of the body

Contents

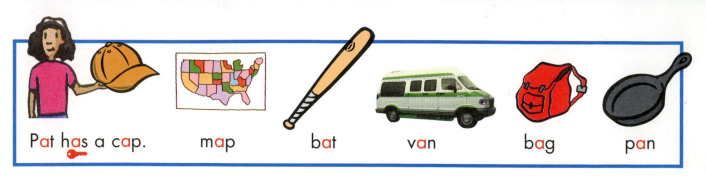

Pat has a cap.　　map　　bat　　van　　bag　　pan

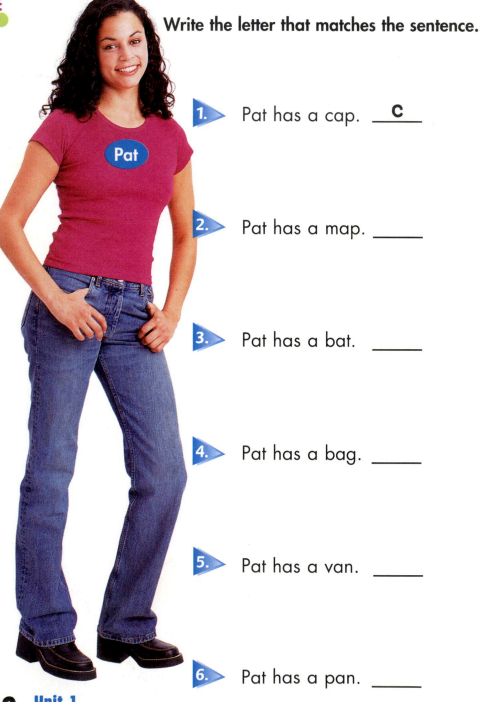

Pat

Write the letter that matches the sentence.

1. ▶ Pat has a cap. ___**c**___

2. ▶ Pat has a map. _____

3. ▶ Pat has a bat. _____

4. ▶ Pat has a bag. _____

5. ▶ Pat has a van. _____

6. ▶ Pat has a pan. _____

a

b

c

d

e

f

man   mat   hat   Pat taps a bat.   A fat cat

Write the word that finishes each sentence.

1. ▶ Pat has a _____**mat**_____ .

2. ▶ Pat has a _____ .

3. ▶ Pat taps a _____ .

4. ▶ Pat has a _____ .

5. ▶ A man has a _____ .

6. ▶ Pat has a _____ .

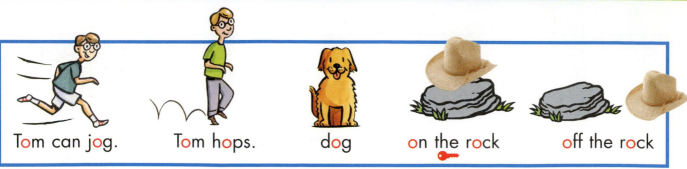

Tom can jog. Tom hops. dog on the rock off the rock

Write the letter that matches the sentence.

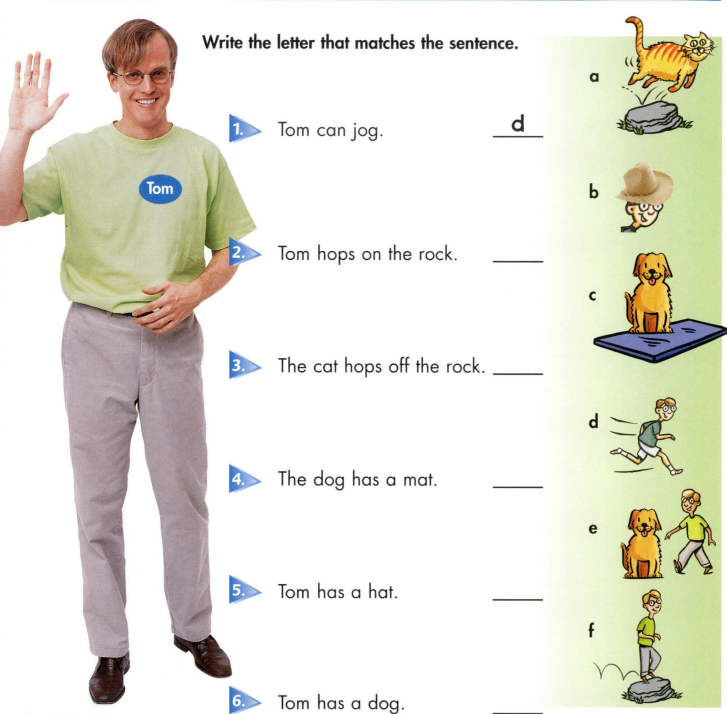

1. Tom can jog. ___d___

2. Tom hops on the rock. _____

3. The cat hops off the rock. _____

4. The dog has a mat. _____

5. Tom has a hat. _____

6. Tom has a dog. _____

a

b

c

d

e

f

Tom **can** jog.   The mop **cannot** jog.   pot

Write the word that finishes each sentence.

1. ▶ The mop _____**cannot**_____ hop.
   can/cannot

2. ▶ Pat _____ jog.
   can/cannot

3. ▶ Tom _____ hop on a rock.
   can/cannot

4. ▶ A van _____ jog.
   can/cannot

5. ▶ A pot _____ hop.
   can/cannot

6. ▶ A bag _____ jog.
   can/cannot

Will sits on a hill.   Will hits the ball.   The hat fits.   Will has a mitt.

Write the letter that matches the sentence.

1. Will can hit. _**b**_

2. Will sits on a mat. _____

3. The hat fits Will. _____

4. A ball is in the mitt. _____

5. A cat sits on a hill. _____

6. A cat sits on the mat. _____

a

b

c

d

e

f

is sad/is not sad   is hot/is not hot

is big/is not big   is bad/is not bad

Write the word or words to match the picture.

1. ▶ Pat ___**is not**___ sad.

is/is not

2. ▶ The pan _____ hot.

is/is not

3. ▶ The van _____ big.

is/is not

4. ▶ The dog _____ bad.

is/is not

5. ▶ The cat _____ big.

is/is not

6. ▶ Tom _____ sad.

is/is not

The bag **of** Will = Will's bag

Match the sentences that mean the same thing.

1. ▷ The hat **of Will** is not big.

2. ▷ The cat **of Pat** is on the mat.

3. ▷ The bag **of Will** is big.

4. ▷ The dog **of Tom** can jog.

a. ◁ **Will's** bag is big.

b. ◁ **Pat's** cat is on the mat.

c. ◁ **Tom's** dog can jog.

d. ◁ **Will's** hat is not big.

On/Off

Write the word to match the picture.

1. ▷ Pat's cap is _____**on**_____ the dog.
on/off

2. ▷ The mitt is _____ the mat.
on/off

3. ▷ Tom is _____ the rock.
on/off

The Big Van

Pat has a big van.
Pat has a map.

The van has Pat's bag and mat in it.
It has a pot and pan in it.
It has a bat and ball in it.

Tom's big dog hops in.
The dog sits in the van.

Pat, Tom, and Will fit in the van.
Tom's big dog fits in the van.
But the box and mitt and pot and
mat cannot fit.

Questions

Circle *yes* if the sentence is true.
Circle *no* if the sentence is not true.

1.	Pat has a van.	(yes)	no
2.	A rock is in the van.	yes	no
3.	Tom has a big map.	yes	no
4.	Pat's bat is in the van.	yes	no
5.	A cat is in the van.	yes	no
6.	Will has a bag.	yes	no
7.	A hat is in the van.	yes	no
8.	A mop is in the van.	yes	no
9.	Tom cannot sit in the van.	yes	no
10.	Tom is a dog.	yes	no

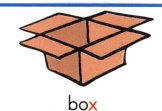		**6**
fo**x**	bo**x**	si**x**

Write the letter that matches the sentence.

1. ▶ The box is big. <u> d </u>

2. ▶ The fox is on the rock. _____

3. ▶ The mitt is in the box. _____

4. ▶ A fox can jog. _____

5. ▶ A six is on the cap. _____

6. ▶ Will has Pat's bag. _____

7. ▶ A box is in the van. _____

8. ▶ The fox is not in the box. _____

a   b

c   d

e   f

g   h

Bud can run.   bus   up   bug   Bud is in the mud.

Write the letter that matches the sentence.

a

1. ▶ Bud can run. ____**b**____

b

2. ▶ The bus is big. _____

c

3. ▶ The van is in the mud. _____

d

4. ▶ Tom runs up a hill. _____

e

5. ▶ Bud is in the box. _____

f

6. ▶ The bug is not big. _____

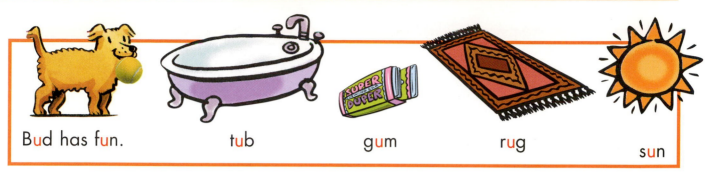

Bud has fun.   tub   gum   rug   sun

Write the word that finishes each sentence.

1. ▶ Bud is in the _____tub_____.

2. ▶ Bud sits on the _____.

3. ▶ Bud runs in the _____.

4. ▶ Bud is in the _____.

5. ▶ Tom has a _____.

6. ▶ The gum is in the _____.

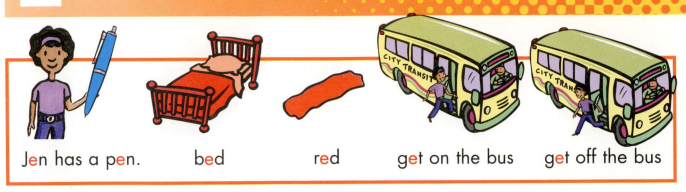

Jen has a pen.   bed   red   get on the bus   get off the bus

Write the letter that matches the sentence.

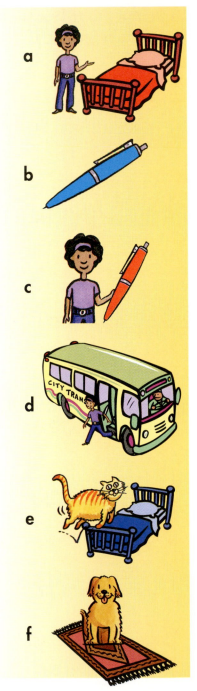

1. Jen has a pen.   __c__

a

2. Jen gets off the bus.   ____

b

3. The cat gets on the bed.   ____

c

4. Jen's bed is red.   ____

d

5. Bud is on the red rug.   ____

e

6. The big pen is red.   ____

f

net   wet dog   egg   seven   leg

Circle *yes* or *no* to answer the questions.

1. Is Jen's leg on the rock?   yes   (no)

2. Is Jen in a van?   yes   no

3. Can a bed run?   yes   no

4. Is the cat wet?   yes   no

5. Is the egg in the pan?   yes   no

6. Is the net up?   yes   no

A Pen

Lots of Pens

Write the word or words to match the picture.

a pen, ~~pens~~

a cat, cats

an egg, eggs

a hat, hats

a bed, beds

a dog, dogs

a leg, legs

a bug, bugs

a bag, bags

a net, nets

1.  **pens**

2.

3.

4.

5.

6.

7.

8.

The Bad Leg

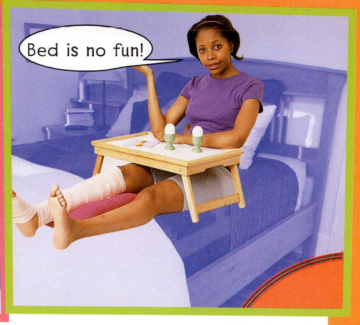

The sun is up.
Tom, Will, and Bud jog up a hill.
A big bus is on the hill.
It hits mud. The mud gets on Bud.

Jen is not up.
Jen cannot run. Jen is in bed.
Jen has a bad leg.
Jen has eggs in bed, but Jen is sad.

Bud runs in.
Bud hops up on Jen's bed.
Bud is all wet.
Mud gets on Jen's leg.

Bud hops off the bed.
The bed has mud on it.
The red rug has mud on it.
Bud runs and sits in the sun.

Questions

Ruff!

| Bud | leg | wet | hill | ~~up~~ | on | sun | bed | run | not |

Choose a word from the box to finish each sentence.

1. ▶ The sun is _____**up**_____.

2. ▶ Jen is _____ up.

3. ▶ Jen is in _____.

4. ▶ The mud hits _____.

5. ▶ Jen has a bad _____.

6. ▶ Tom and Will jog up the _____.

7. ▶ Jen cannot _____.

8. ▶ The dog is all _____.

9. ▶ Bud hops _____ Jen's bed.

10. ▶ Bud runs and sits in the _____.

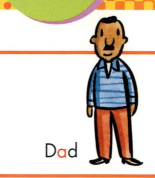

Dad

Mom

Sis

Write the letter that matches the sentence.

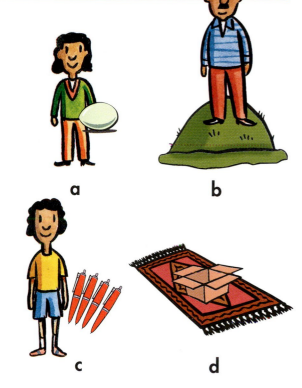

a

b

1. Dad is on the hill. **b**

2. Mom has an egg. _____

3. Sis has a mitt. _____

c

d

4. A bug is in the box. _____

5. Jen cannot run. _____

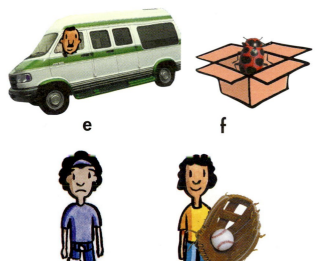

e

f

6. Sis has lots of red pens. _____

7. A box is on the rug. _____

g

h

8. Dad is in the van. _____

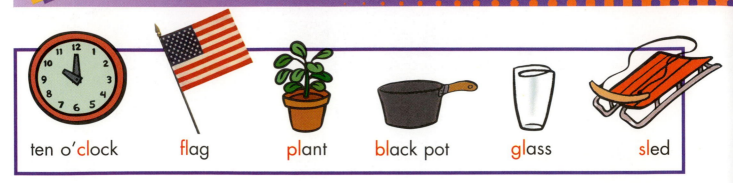

| ten o'clock | flag | plant | black pot | glass | sled |

● **Write the letter that matches the sentence.**

1. Pat has a flag. **b**

a

2. The plant is on a black mat. _____

b

3. The glass is not red. _____

c

4. The plant is in the sun. _____

d

5. The sled is not black. _____

e

6. It is ten o'clock. _____

f

Circle *yes* if the sentence matches the picture.
Circle *no* if it does not.

1. ▶ Bud is in the class.   (yes)   no

2. ▶ A bus is in the class.   yes   no

3. ▶ Bud has a red bag.   yes   no

4. ▶ The bag is black.   yes   no

5. ▶ Tom yells, "Come on, Bud!"   yes   no

6. ▶ A pen is on the plant.   yes   no

7. ▶ Bud has a plant.   yes   no

8. ▶ Bud is a black dog.   yes   no

9. ▶ A flag is in the class.   yes   no

10. ▶ It is ten o'clock.   yes   no

On the Grass

grass   frog   bricks   pick-up truck   crab   dress

Write the letter that matches the sentence.

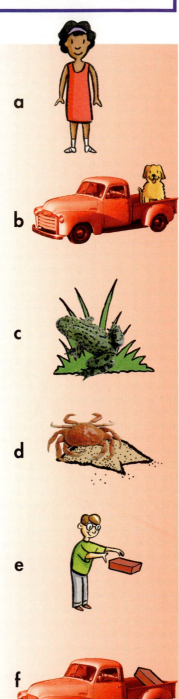

a

b

c

d

e

f

1. The frog is on the grass. ___c___

2. The crab is not on the grass. _____

3. Jen has a red dress. _____

4. Tom drops a red brick. _____

5. A brick is in the pick-up truck. _____

6. Bud is in the pick-up truck. _____

On the Steps

spill

swim

smell

steps

snack

Tom's skin is hot.

Write the letter that matches the sentence.

1. A big stick is on the steps. __e__

2. The skin on Tom's leg is hot. _____

3. The glass spills. _____

4. The bus has steps. _____

5. Will can swim. _____

6. Pat can smell the snack. _____

a

b

c

d

e

f

On the Sand

sand   Tom drinks his milk.   jump   gift

Write the word that finishes each sentence.

1. Bud runs on the __**sand**__ .

2. A frog can _____ on a rock.

3. Jen has a glass of _____ .

4. Will has a _____ .

5. Tom _____ his milk.

6. Will can _____ .

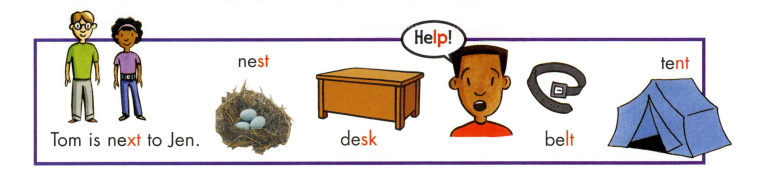

nest

Help!

tent

Tom is next to Jen.   desk   belt

Write the word that finishes each sentence.

1. ▶ The frog is ___**next**___ to the rock.

2. ▶ Jen's dress has a black _____.

3. ▶ Bud is next to the _____.

4. ▶ The _____ has eggs in it.

5. ▶ Will yells, "_____!"

6. ▶ Pat sits at a _____.

Circle *yes* if the question matches the picture.
Circle *no* if it does not.

1. ▶ Is the gas pump next to the pick-up truck?   (yes)   no

2. ▶ Is a man in the truck?   yes   no

3. ▶ Is a man next to the truck?   yes   no

4. ▶ Is a dog on the grass?   yes   no

5. ▶ Is a fan belt on the grass?   yes   no

6. ▶ Is Jen next to the truck?   yes   no

7. ▶ Is a cat on the gas pump?   yes   no

8. ▶ Is a desk in the truck?   yes   no

9. ▶ Is a brick in the truck?   yes   no

10. ▶ Is a van next to the gas pump?   yes   no

The Truck

Tom gets up at six o'clock.
The clock is next to the bed.
Tom puts his pants and belt on.
Tom has a job at seven o'clock.

Tom gets eggs and a glass of milk.
Tom drops the glass. The milk spills.
Tom runs to get his snack.
His snack is in a bag.
Tom has to get to his job!

Tom jogs up the steps to his truck.
Bud runs next to Tom.
The red pick-up truck is on the grass.
It has bricks, plants, sticks, and
sand in it.
Tom jumps in the truck.

The truck runs and stops.
It runs and stops and runs and stops.
Is it the gas? Is it the fan belt?
Tom yells at the truck.
It is seven o'clock.
Can Tom get to his job?

Questions

Number the sentences 1–10 in the order they happened in the story.

1. ▷ Tom jumps in his truck. _____

2. ▷ The truck runs and stops. _____

3. ▷ Tom gets up at six o'clock. <u>1</u>

4. ▷ It is 7:00 and Tom cannot get to his job. _____

5. ▷ Tom puts his pants and belt on. _____

6. ▷ Tom yells, "Come on, truck!" _____

7. ▷ Tom jogs up the steps. _____

8. ▷ Tom gets eggs and a glass of milk. _____

9. ▷ The truck is on the grass. _____

10. ▷ Tom runs to get his snack. _____

Blends and Short Vowels

~~dog~~	grass	bus	pens	hit
desk	class	run	dress	sits

Self Test: Write the word that finishes each sentence.

1. Bud is a big _____dog_____ .

2. Will can _____ the ball.

3. Bud and Tom can _____ .

4. Pat and Tom get on the _____ .

5. Jen has ten red _____ .

6. A frog hops in the _____ .

7. A plant is on the _____ .

8. A flag is in the _____ .

9. Will _____ on a hill.

10. Jen has a red _____ .

May takes a plate.

May makes a cake.

May wakes up.

waves in a lake

snake and grapes

Write the letter that matches the sentence.

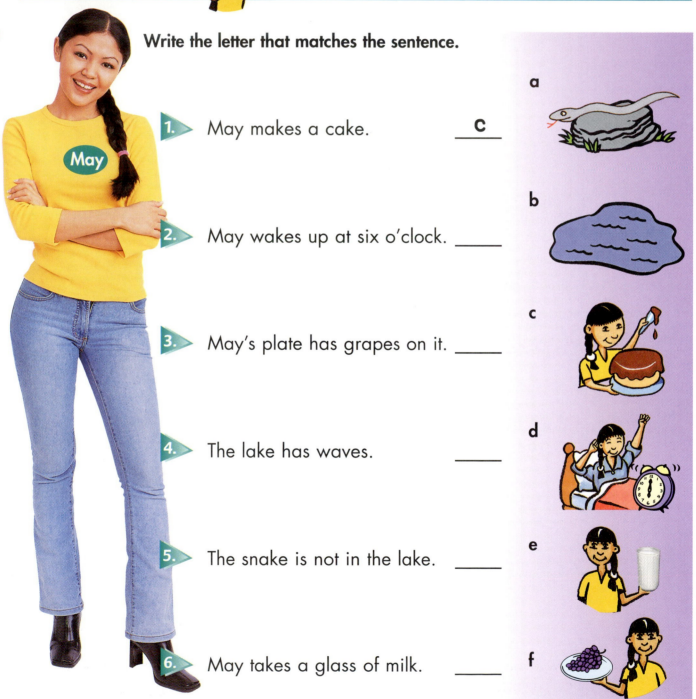

1. May makes a cake. _____c_____

2. May wakes up at six o'clock. _____

3. May's plate has grapes on it. _____

4. The lake has waves. _____

5. The snake is not in the lake. _____

6. May takes a glass of milk. _____

a

b

c

d

e

f

May plays.

Hey, May!

May plays on a gray day.

Tom and Pat say, "Hey, May!"

May lays a tray on the table.

Write the word that finishes each sentence.

1. May and Bud ____**play**____.
say/play

2. May takes a _____ plate.
gray/red

3. May lays a _____ on the table.
tray/snake

4. Tom and Pat _____, "Hey!"
play/say

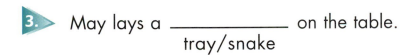

5. May _____ up at ten o'clock.
makes/wakes

6. The _____ is on the tray.
cake/lake

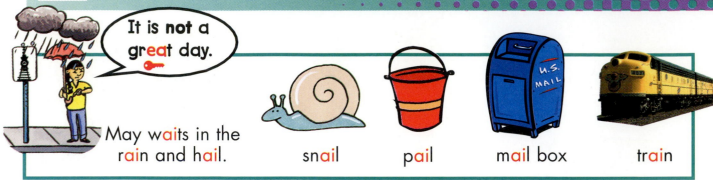

It is **not** a gr**ea**t day.

May w**ai**ts in the r**ai**n and h**ai**l.

sn**ai**l

p**ai**l

m**ai**l box

tr**ai**n

Write the letter that matches the sentence.

a

1. ▷ May waits for the train in the rain. __d__

2. ▷ May takes the red pail away. ____

b

3. ▷ May gets on the train at eight. ____

c

4. ▷ "The day is great!" says May. ____

d

5. ▷ Rain falls on the mail box. ____

e

6. ▷ Hail lands on the snail. ____

f

ace age   May's Face on the Page

May's face is on the page.   May and Pat race.   cage   stage

Circle *yes* if the sentence matches the pictures above.
Circle *no* if it does not.

1. ▶ May has a sad face.   yes   (no)

2. ▶ The page has a face on it.   yes   no

3. ▶ May and Bud race on the grass.   yes   no

4. ▶ May is on the stage.   yes   no

The page has.../Lots of pages have...

Write the word that finishes each sentence.

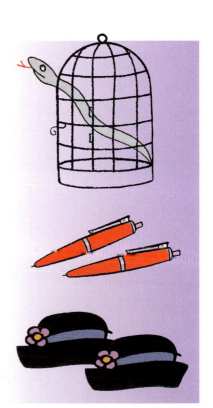

1. ▶ The cage **has** a ___snake___ in it.

2. ▶ Will and Tom **have** red _____.

3. ▶ May and Pat **have** black _____.

It's the same.

it is	=	it's
is not	=	isn't 🔑
cannot	=	can't
let us	=	let's

Match the sentences that mean the same.

1. ▶ **It is** a great day.

2. ▶ A snake **cannot** make a cake.

3. ▶ **Let us** take a snack.

4. ▶ The snail **is not** in the pail.

a. ▶ **Let's** take a snack.

b. ▶ **It's** a great day.

c. ▶ The snail **isn't** in the pail.

d. ▶ A snake **can't** make a cake.

Two words can mean almost the same.

Read the first sentence. Finish the second sentence with
the word that means almost the same.

1. ▶ A frog can **hop**. = A frog can ___**jump**___ .
jump/walk 🔑

2. ▶ Tom can **jog**. = Tom can _____ .
swim/run

3. ▶ May has a **picnic**. = May has a _____ .
snack/snake

A Day at the Lake

Names in the play: May, Pat, Will, Tom, Narrator

Narrator: *The sun is up. It's a great day. May calls Pat.*

May: Hey, wake up, Pat! It's eight o'clock.

Pat: Is it eight?

May: Yes, get up! Let's have a picnic at the lake.

Pat: Great! Let's call Will, Jen, and Tom.

May: And Bud! Let's take the dog.

Pat: Tom can take the truck.

May: Tom can't take the truck. It stops.

Pat: Okay. Let's take the van.

Narrator: *Will sits on the steps. May calls Will.*

May: Hey, Will! Let's have a picnic at the lake today.

Will: Great! Can Pat take the van?

May: Yes. But Tom can't take his truck.

Will: Can Jen make a snack?

May: Yes. Jen has the snack and the drinks. Tom and Pat have the grapes and the cake.

Will: Wait. Can Jen get the plates?

May: Pat has the plates in the van.

Will: Okay.

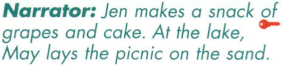

Narrator: *Jen makes a snack of grapes and cake. At the lake, May lays the picnic on the sand.*

Tom: Wait, May! A snail is on the plate.

May: It's not a snail. It's a big grape.

Tom: No, it's not. It's a snail!

Will: Come on. The snail can wait. Let's swim.

May: No. The lake has gray waves.

Pat: Let's walk next to the lake.

Tom: No. Let's play ball.

May and Pat: Okay. Great!

Narrator: *Tom, May, and Pat play a ball game. Bud takes a stick and runs in the waves. But is it a stick?*

May: Hey, get the dog! Bud has a stick!

Tom: Is it a stick?

Pat: No, it's a snake!

Tom: Bud, drop the snake!

Pat: Drop the snake, Bud!

Tom: Jump on it, Pat.

Pat: No. It's big!

Narrator: *The snake gets away. Bud runs on the sand. The day gets gray. Rain falls on the picnic. Jen, Pat, Tom, and Will run to the van.*

May: It is *not* a great day!

Questions

Circle *yes* if the sentence matches the picture.
Circle *no* if it does not.

1. ▶ May, Tom, and Pat play a game on the sand.   (yes)   no

2. ▶ Rain lands on the grapes.   yes   no

3. ▶ Tom swims in the waves.   yes   no

4. ▶ A snail is on the plate.   yes   no

5. ▶ Pat and Tom have a race.   yes   no

6. ▶ The cake is next to the grapes.   yes   no

7. ▶ May's face is sad.   yes   no

8. ▶ The lake is gray.   yes   no

9. ▶ Tom has a snake.   yes   no

10. ▶ Bud has a stick.   yes   no

Mike rides a bike.

Mike likes pie.

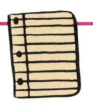
nine lines

Mike drives five miles.

NEXT 5 MILES

Write the letter that matches the sentence.

a

1. Mike rides in the rain. __e__

b

2. Mike has five pens. ____

c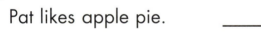

3. Pat likes apple pie. ____

d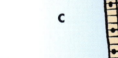

4. Mike drives five miles. ____

e

5. The time is five past nine. ____

6. The page has nine lines. ____

f

Mike

I -y I like my bike.

Hi! I am Mike. My bike is fast.

eyes / smile

A plane can fly in the sky.

cry / cries

Write the word that finishes each sentence.

Mike's Bike

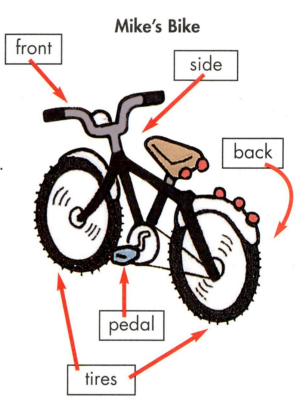

front

side

back

pedal

tires

1. ▶ Mike says, "_____My_____ bike is fast."

2. ▶ A bike has _____ in front and back.

3. ▶ Mike says, "Hi! _____ am Mike."

4. ▶ A bike is not like a plane.

   A plane can _____ in the sky.

5. ▶ Mike's face is not sad.

   It has a big _____.

6. ▶ Mike stops and _____, "Yikes!"

Yikes!

STOP

br**igh**t l**igh**t at n**igh**t

The plane flies h**igh**.

left hand/r**igh**t hand

Write the word that finishes each sentence.

1. Mike has a bright ___**light**___ on his bike.

2. Mike can ride the bike at _____.

3. A big _____ is on the front of Mike's bike.

4. The light of the sun is _____.

5. A plane flies _____ in the sky.

6. The light is in Mike's _____ hand.

ire · ice   Fire and Ice

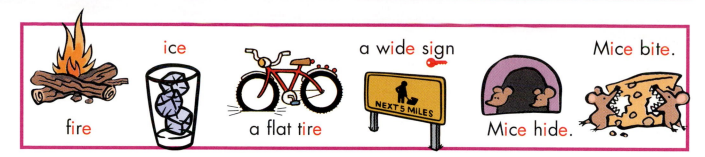

fire · ice · a flat tire · a wide sign · Mice hide. · Mice bite.

Circle _yes_ if the sentence is true.
Circle _no_ if the sentence is not true.

1. A fire is hot.   (yes)   no

2. Mice can fly in the sky.   yes   no

3. A stop sign is red.   yes   no

4. Ice is hot.   yes   no

5. A dog can bite a ball.   yes   no

6. A sign can bite a light.   yes   no

7. Bikes have nine tires.   yes   no

8. A frog can hide in the grass.   yes   no

9. A pen is wide and big.   yes   no

10. A flat tire can make a bike stop.   yes   no

11. Mice can drive a truck.   yes   no

12. A fire is bright.   yes   no

Rhymes

Rhymes have the same ending sounds.
Example: *Mike* and *like* rhyme.

~~lake~~	face	man	night
sky	tire	hot	run	train
bag	day	page	wide
sand	snail	class	nine	jog

Read the word. Find a word from the box above that rhymes with it.
Write the rhyming word on the line.

1. take __lake__

2. hand _____

3. ride _____

4. race _____

5. van _____

6. flag _____

7. fly _____

8. fire _____

9. line _____

10. dog _____

11. not _____

12. cage _____

13. sun _____

14. rain _____

15. light _____

16. play _____

17. grass _____

18. pail _____

The Bike Race

Come on, Tom! The bike race is today.

I can't race today, Mike. I have a job.

I like to race. My bike is fast.

Just wait! My bike can fly.

Today is the five-mile race. Mike and Jen can't wait to race. Mike calls Tom, but Tom cannot race today.

Mike and Jen get to the race. Jen's bright red bike is on the line. Mike's black bike is next to Jen's. The man drops the flag. The race is on!

Hey, Jen! A rock! Stop!

Yikes! I can't!

Is the leg okay, Jen?

Yes. It's fine. But my front tire is flat.

Oh, well. Next time.

Nine bikes race on the hill. Mike is in front. Jen flies past Mike. Mike cries to Jen.

Mike stops to help Jen. Seven bikes race past. Jen's tire is flat, but Jen is okay.

Questions

~~mile~~	job
rock	fly
nine	help
red	wait
black	tire

Complete the sentences below using a word from the box.

1. ▶ The bike race is a five-_____**mile**_____ race.

2. ▶ Mike and Jen can't _____ to race.

3. ▶ Mike calls Tom, but Tom has a _____ and can't race.

4. ▶ Mike has a _____ bike.

5. ▶ Jen has a bright _____ bike.

6. ▶ _____ bikes race on the hill.

7. ▶ Jen says, "My bike can _____."

8. ▶ Jen's bike hits a _____.

9. ▶ Jen's bike has a flat _____.

10. ▶ Mike stops to _____ Jen.

To discuss:

- Is Mike right to stop and help Jen?
- Can Jen ride on a flat tire?
- Can Tom have a job and race on the same day?

My Life

Write about yourself.

1. ▶ My name is _____ .

                                     name

2. ▶ My address is _____ .

                                     address

Mike Pace
777 Red Sands Lane
Dayton, OH 45390

_____ .

3. ▶ My age is _____ .

                                     age

4. ▶ My mom's name is _____ .

                                     Mom's name

5. ▶ My dad's name is _____ .

                                     Dad's name

6. ▶ I have: __**X**__ a pen   _____ a van   _____ a job

               _____ a car   _____ a truck   _____ a bike

               _____ a dog   _____ a cat   _____ a desk

7. ▶ I like to: _____ jog   _____ walk

               _____ play baseball   _____ have a picnic on the sand

               _____ get up at nine o'clock   _____ ride a bike

               _____ swim   _____ get up at six o'clock

8. ▶ A snack I like is: _____ grapes   _____ milk

                       _____ hot dogs   _____ pie

                       _____ cake   _____ (*other*)

Joe's nose

Joe's boat can float.

Goat on a road

soap

SOAP

stove

Write the letter that matches the sentence.

1. Joe has an old boat. ___d___

2. Joe holds the soap. _____

3. Joe has glasses on his nose. _____

4. The bus goes on the road. _____

5. The goat has a rope on its nose. _____

6. An old pan is on the stove. _____

a

b

c

d

e

f

o ow Go Fast/Go Slow

fast boat/slow boat yellow coat Roses grow. Winds blow. cold snow stop/go

Write the word that finishes each sentence.

1. ▶ A rowboat is a __**slow**__ boat.

2. ▶ Joe walks in the _____ and gets cold.

3. ▶ Cold winds _____ in the tree.

4. ▶ Joe has a _____ coat.

5. ▶ Roses _____ in the sun.

6. ▶ The light says the bus can _____.

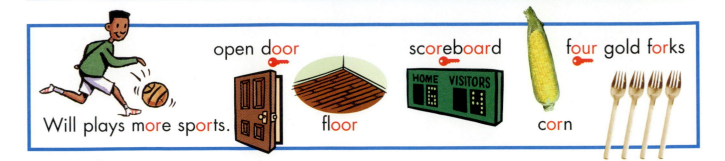

open door   scoreboard   four gold forks

Will plays more sports.   floor   corn

Circle *yes* if the sentence is true.
Circle *no* if it is not.

1.	Basketball is a sport.	(yes)	no
2.	Tennis is a sport.	yes	no
3.	Boats can play basketball.	yes	no
4.	Baseball is a sport.	yes	no
5.	A scoreboard has a score on it.	yes	no
6.	Forks can run on a plate.	yes	no
7.	Corn is yellow.	yes	no
8.	A rowboat can fly.	yes	no
9.	Wind can blow a door open.	yes	no
10.	Grass grows on a floor.	yes	no
11.	A goat has four noses.	yes	no
12.	A van has doors.	yes	no

High and *low* are opposites.

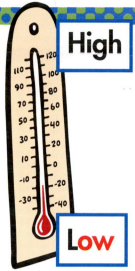

High

Low

~~low~~	is	slow	cold
no	rain	day	hold
on	sad	big	cannot
back	ice	ride	go

**Find the word in the box that is the opposite of the one below.
Write it on the line.**

1. high __low__

2. little _____

3. yes _____

4. hot _____

5. can _____

6. is not _____

7. front _____

8. stop _____

9. off _____

10. fast _____

11. sun _____

12. drop _____

13. night _____

14. happy _____

15. walk _____

16. fire _____

e–e ea ee   Steve reads and sleeps.

He sleeps by a tree.

Steve reads. ←leaf   The team eats meat.

green beans and peas

feet

Write the letter that matches the sentence.

1. ▶ Steve reads by a tree. ___b___

 a

2. ▶ Steve has no socks on his feet. ____

 b

3. ▶ He is on the green team. ____

 c

4. ▶ Steve eats green beans. ____

 d

5. ▶ Bud eats Steve's meat. ____

 e

6. ▶ Steve sleeps till nine o'clock. ____

 f

50 **Unit 6**
Long Vowels: /ē/ e–e, ea, ee; Verbs: read, sleep, eat

ie The Baseball Field

above

in back of   behind

fence   Umpire

below

in front of   Steve

Pat

beside   by

Jen   Tom

Mike

Will   May   between

Circle *yes* if the sentence matches the picture.
Circle *no* if it does not.

1. ▶ Jen is beside Mike.   (yes)   no

2. ▶ The flag is above the field.   yes   no

3. ▶ Pat is in front of Steve.   yes   no

4. ▶ The fence is behind the umpire.   yes   no

5. ▶ The umpire is in back of a tree.   yes   no

6. ▶ A boat is above the flag.   yes   no

7. ▶ May is between Tom and Will.   yes   no

8. ▶ Steve is by home plate.   yes   no

9. ▶ A goat is below the tree.   yes   no

10. ▶ Pat is in front of the umpire.   yes   no

Sorry.

60-40=20

key funn**y** monk**ey** happ**y** bab**y** He has to stud**y**. Sixty minus fort**y** is twent**y**.

Write the word or words from above that answer the riddle.

1. ▶ A hand can hold it. It is little. It makes a door easy to open. It is a _____**key**_____.

2. ▶ It is a sport. A team plays it on ice. The team has sticks. It is _____.

3. ▶ It is the same as sixty minus forty. It is _____.

4. ▶ He cannot go to a game. He has a test and has to _____.

5. ▶ He smiles a lot. He likes milk. He plays on a mat. He is a _____.

6. ▶ He plays in trees. He can jump high. He has feet and hands. He likes bananas. He is a _____.

 A deer is near.

 Steve's ears can hear.

 Eyes can see. tears

 He is nineteen years old.

 beard

Write the word that finishes each sentence.

1. The _____**deer**_____ is near Steve.

2. Steve's eyes can _____ the deer.

3. The deer's ears can _____ Steve.

4. Joe has a gray _____.

5. Joe is sixty _____ old.

6. Steve is sad. He has _____ in his eyes.

u | ue | u–e Luz has a blue flute.

Luz plays a tune on the flute.

music

Luz uses the glue.

The sky is blue in June.

a huge cube

Write the letter that matches the sentence.

Luz

a

1. ▶ Luz has a blue flute. **c**

b

2. ▶ A rainy sky is not blue. ____

3. ▶ Luz reads lines of music. ____

c

d

4. ▶ Luz uses the glue. ____

5. ▶ The glass has ice cubes in it. ____

e

6. ▶ Luz likes roses in June. ____

f

54 **Unit 6**
Long Vowels: /ü/ue, u-e; Verb: use, play; Adjectives: blue, huge

ou | **Do you...?**

Circle *yes* if you do. Circle *no* if you do not.

1. ▶ Do you like fruit? ⟨Yes, I do.⟩ No, I don't.

2. ▶ Do you like grape juice? Yes, I do. No, I don't.

3. ▶ Do you like to play baseball? Yes, I do. No, I don't.

4. ▶ Do you walk to class? Yes, I do. No, I don't.

5. ▶ Do you have a job? Yes, I do. No, I don't.

6. ▶ Do you drive? Yes, I do. No, I don't.

7. ▶ Do you ride the bus? Yes, I do. No, I don't.

8. ▶ Do you help at home? Yes, I do. No, I don't.

9. ▶ Do you play basketball? Yes, I do. No, I don't.

10. ▶ Do you sit in the front of the class? Yes, I do. No, I don't.

11. ▶ Do you play music? Yes, I do. No, I don't.

12. ▶ Do you get up at 7:00? Yes, I do. No, I don't.

ew | Old/New | Many/Few

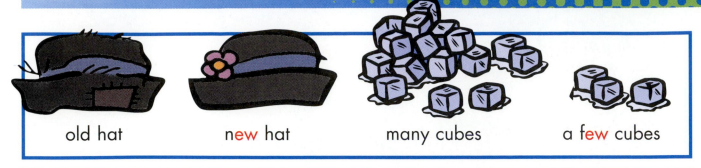

| old hat | new hat | many cubes | a few cubes |

~~few~~	sunny	happy	low	behind	sleep	day	hot
ride	do	hold	get on	wait	huge	above	fast

Find the word from the box above that is opposite to the one below.
Write it on the line.

1. ▶ many ___few___

2. ▶ sad _____

3. ▶ high _____

4. ▶ rainy _____

5. ▶ below _____

6. ▶ drop _____

7. ▶ don't _____

8. ▶ cold _____

9. ▶ in front of _____

10. ▶ night _____

11. ▶ little _____

12. ▶ go _____

13. ▶ wake up _____

14. ▶ walk _____

15. ▶ get off _____

16. ▶ slow _____

Home Run

Names in the play: Luz, Pat, Mike, Jen, Steve, Tom, Will, May, Umpire, Narrator

Narrator: The green team is at bat. Luz, Pat, and Mike have hits and wait on the bases. Steve steps up to the plate.

Jen: Go, Steve!

May: You can do it, Steve!

Steve: Okay. [*to Jen*] Can you see the big tree?

Jen: You mean the tree behind the fence?

Steve: Right.

Jen: Yes, I see it. Can you hit it?

Steve: Easy. Wait and see.

Jen: Do it, Steve! Hit the tree!

May: Go for it, Steve!

Narrator: The blue team waits in the field. Steve taps his bat.

Umpire: Ball one.

Tom: Wide and low.

Will: Let the low ones go, Steve.

Narrator: A slow ball floats in low.

Umpire: Ball two!

Will: Wait for the right one, Steve!

Jen: Yes, wait for a high one.

Steve: Come on. Let's have it. Time for a fast ball.

Umpire: Strike one!

Narrator: *Steve leaves the box. He taps the bat and faces the plate.*

Umpire: Play ball!

Will: You can do it, Steve.

Jen: Hit it away, Steve.

Umpire: Strike two!

May: Oh, no! Two strikes.

Will: And two balls. Four balls and he walks in a run.

Mike: Hit me in, Steve!

Narrator: *The ball comes in fast. Steve steps up. He hits a high fly.*

Will: Come on home, Mike! Run, Pat! Run, Luz!

Narrator: *The ball floats high above the field. It goes past the fence and lands … in the tree.*

May: It's in the tree. Run, Steve! You hit the tree!

Umpire: SAFE!

Jen: It's a home run! Come on in, Pat!

Umpire: SAFE!

Narrator: *Luz runs past two bases, down the line and jumps on home plate. Steve jogs in. His hands go up high and a smile is on his face.*

Pat: See the scoreboard? Six-to-five.

All the team: We win! Let's hear it for the green team!

Questions

~~green~~	low	slow
tree	wide	ball
plate	strikes	field
floats	go	by
home	wait	blue

Use ten words from the box to finish the sentences.

1. ▷ The _____**green**_____ team is at bat.

2. ▷ The blue team is in the _____.

3. ▷ Steve steps up to the _____ and taps his bat.

4. ▷ May says, "_____ for it, Steve!"

5. ▷ Ball one is _____ and low.

6. ▷ Will yells, "_____ for the right one, Steve!"

7. ▷ Steve gets two balls and two _____.

8. ▷ Steve hits the fast ball and it _____ high above the field.

9. ▷ The ball lands in the big _____ behind the fence.

10. ▷ Jen cries, "It's a _____ run!"

sh | **Sh**e likes to **sh**op.

She **sh**ops for **sh**oes.

shoes

She wa**sh**es di**sh**es.

bru**sh** on a **sh**elf

fi**sh**

He **sh**aves.

Write the letter that matches the sentence.

1. ▶ She shops for new black shoes. ___d___

2. ▶ Four sheep eat grass. _____

3. ▶ He wakes up at 6:00 and shaves. _____

4. ▶ Wash your hands before you eat. _____

5. ▶ The dish has a fish on it. _____

6. ▶ A belt is on the shelf. _____

a

b

c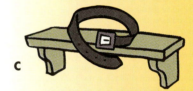

d

e

f

tele**ph**one

ear**ph**ones

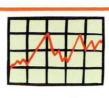
gra**ph**

Phonics Team **ph**oto

ele**ph**ant

Fill in the phone conversation. Write the words that finish each sentence.

Steve: Hi, Mike.

Mike: Hi, Steve.

Steve: Do you want to play _____ **baseball** _____?
baseball / brush

Mike: Sure. Do you have your new _____?
graph / bat

Steve: Yes. Do you have your _____?
mitt / fish

Mike: Yes. Let's phone May to see if _____ can play.
she / he

Steve: She has to baby-sit. She _____ play.
can / can't

Mike: Okay. Let's play on the _____ next to your road.
field / photo

Steve: Fine. Can you ride your _____ here?
earphones / bike

Mike: Sure. See you in ten minutes.

Steve: Okay. Bye, Mike.

Mike: Bye.

math
2a + 4a = 3b
a = ?

thick/thin   thumb   throw   bath   May thinks.   three months

Circle *yes* if the sentence is true. Circle *no* if the sentence is not true. If the old sentence is not true, write a new one that *is* true. Copy the true sentence.

1. ▶ A leaf is thick and black.   yes   (no)

   __A leaf is thin and green._____

2. ▶ Math problems make you think.   yes   no

   _____

3. ▶ A hand has six thumbs.   yes   no

   _____

4. ▶ A baby likes to splash in the bath.   yes   no

   _____

5. ▶ A man can throw an elephant.   yes   no

   _____

6. ▶ A year has three months.   yes   no

   _____

Write the word that finishes each sentence.

1. Will plays a game of ____baseball____ *with* Mike.

2. Pat fishes in the _____ *with* Joe.

3. Tom dashes on the _____ *with* Jen.

4. Luz sits *with* Steve and plays a _____.

5. May is on the grass *with* the _____.

6. Bud runs away *with* Will's _____.

7. The van is by the grass *with* the _____.

8. A _____ jumps and makes a splash *with* its tail.

th **Th**is _____ rhymes with **th**at _____.

Sheep sleep.

Read the word on **this** side. Then write the rhyme from **that** side.

1. ▶ dish   **fish** _____

2. ▶ dash _____

3. ▶ that _____

4. ▶ new _____

5. ▶ shake _____

6. ▶ shop _____

7. ▶ coat _____

8. ▶ throw _____

9. ▶ bath _____

10. ▶ sheep _____

11. ▶ nine _____

12. ▶ three _____

13. ▶ boat _____

14. ▶ rose _____

grow

stop

math

nose

tree

~~fish~~

hat

float

line

make

splash

few

boat

sleep

Bath Time for Baby

Be sure to give the baby a bath at six thirty, May.

Okay, Mrs. Roth.

Okay, Baby Beth. Let's wash your little thumbs and toes. Let's wash your little ears and eyes.

Ma, ma, ga, ga.

ring!

Mrs. Roth phones May to baby-sit for Baby Beth. May comes to the Roth home at three o'clock. She thinks this job is fun.

Baby Beth is in the bathtub. She splashes and plays with a little fish. May hears the phone. It is on the shelf near the bathtub.

Hi, May. Do you want to go to the movies with Mike and me?

No, I can't, Will. I have to baby-sit till nine o'clock. This is a bad time. Sorry, I have to go.

Don't eat the phone, Baby Beth! You can have a snack before you go to bed.

Ga ga, ba ba!

May picks up the phone. She talks to Will and holds the baby. Baby Beth throws the little fish on the floor and tries to take the phone.

May dries the baby, but little Beth shakes the phone and tries to eat it. May gives Baby Beth a snack and reads to the baby. At last little Beth sleeps.

Questions

~~thinks~~	shakes
phone	movies
fish	Beth
bathtub	wash
Roth	throws

Complete the sentences below using a word from the box.

1. May _____**thinks**_____ this job is fun.

2. May says, "Okay, Baby Beth. Let's _____ your little thumbs and toes."

3. Mrs. _____ is the baby's mom.

4. The baby plays with a little _____.

5. The baby's name is _____.

6. She _____ the fish on the floor.

7. The baby _____ the phone and tries to eat it.

8. Baby Beth sits in the _____ and splashes.

9. Will says, "Do you want to go to the _____ with Mike and me?"

10. May says, "Don't eat the _____ , Baby Beth!"

To discuss:

- Do you baby-sit?
- Do you have a job?
- Do you go to the movies? Name the movies you like.

These Clothes, Those Clothes

These shoes are blue.

Those shoes are red.

Which of **these** clothes go with **those** clothes?
Match the clothes that are the same colors. Write your answers.

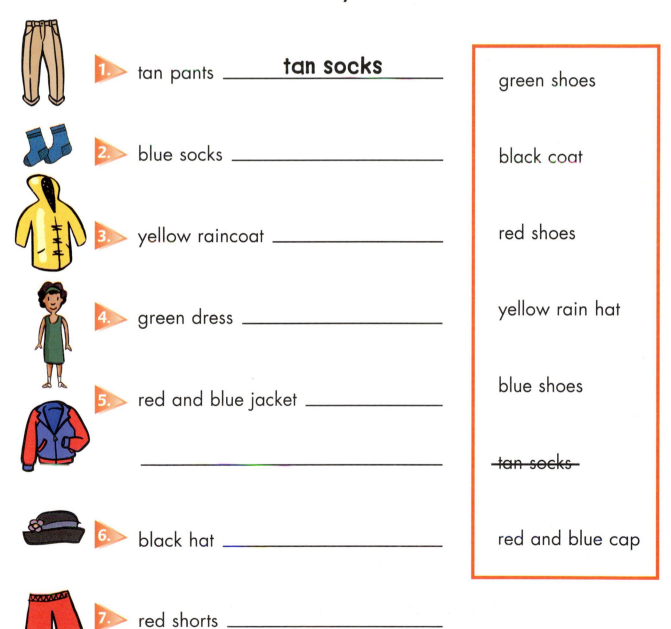

1. tan pants ___tan socks___

2. blue socks _____

3. yellow raincoat _____

4. green dress _____

5. red and blue jacket _____

_____

6. black hat _____

7. red shorts _____

green shoes

black coat

red shoes

yellow rain hat

blue shoes

~~tan socks~~

red and blue cap

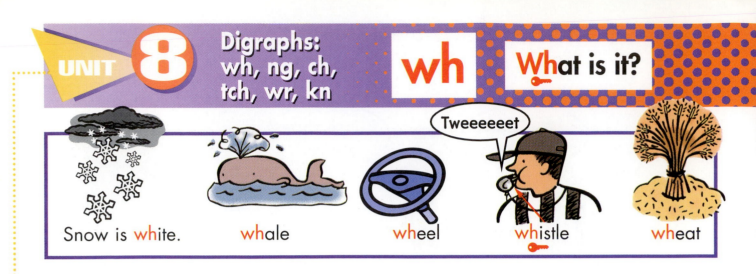

Snow is white.   whale   wheel   whistle   wheat

Tweeeeeet

Draw a line to the sentence that answers the question.

1. What is a whale?

2. What is a wheel?

3. What is wheat?

4. What is a whistle?

5. What is snow?

6. What is a dish?

7. What is a bathtub?

8. What is a shelf?

a. It is a grain that you use to make bread.

b. It is a huge animal that swims in the sea.

c. It falls from the sky in cold, white flakes.

d. It is the same as a plate.

e. It is a big object that you sit in to wash yourself.

f. It is a little object that you blow to stop a game.

g. It is a flat place for brushes and dishes.

h. It is what your hands use to drive a truck.

wh | When?

1	**2**	**3**	**4**	**5**	**6**	**7**	**8**	**9**	**10**
one	two	three	four	five	six	seven	eight	nine	ten

11	**12**	**13**	**14**	**15**	**16**	**17**	**18**
eleven	twelve	thirteen	fourteen	fifteen	sixteen	seventeen	eighteen

19	**20**	**21**	**22**	**23**	**24**	**25**
nineteen	twenty	twenty-one	twenty-two	twenty-three	twenty-four	twenty-five

26	**27**	**28**	**29**	**30**	**40**	**50**	**60**
twenty-six	twenty-seven	twenty-eight	twenty-nine	thirty	forty	fifty	sixty

Write the time in numbers. Then write the words from the box above that stand for your numbers.

1. ▷ When do you wake up? I wake up at **6:30** **six thirty** .
   (numbers)   (words)

2. ▷ When do you wash your face? I wash at _____ _____ .

3. ▷ When do you go to class? I go to class at _____ _____ .

4. ▷ When do you have a snack? I have a snack at _____ _____ .

5. ▷ When is your last class? My last class is at _____ _____ .

6. ▷ When do you go back home? I go home at _____ _____ .

7. ▷ When do you study? I study at _____ _____ .

8. ▷ When do you go to bed? I go to bed at _____ _____ .

ng Sing a song.

Luz si**ng**s a so**ng**.   a ki**ng** with a ri**ng**   a lo**ng** stri**ng**   hu**ng**ry

Write the word that finishes each sentence.

1. Luz _____**sings**_____ a new song.

sings/sleeps

2. The whistle is on a long _____.

string/king

3. A _____ is music that you sing.

song/string

4. The king has a big _____ on his hand.

ring/string

5. Pat is _____ and she wants to eat.

happy/hungry

6. A snake is _____ and thin.

song/long

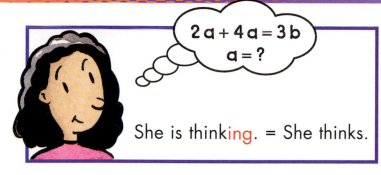

$$2a + 4a = 3b$$
$$a = ?$$

She is thinking. = She thinks.

Write the letter that matches the sentence.

1. Luz is singing a song.   __h__

2. Steve is reading.   _____

3. Jen is washing the dishes. _____

4. Will is swimming.   _____

5. Mike is riding a bike.   _____

6. Steve is sleeping.   _____

7. Bud is eating the meat.   _____

8. The frog is jumping.   _____

9. May is taking a plate.   _____

10. Tom is jogging.   _____

a   b

c   d

e   f

g   h

i   j

ch Cheese for Lunch

cheese   sandwich   lunchbox   chicken   peach   check

Write the word that finishes each sentence.

1. ▶ Steve has cheese in his _____**sandwich**_____ .

2. ▶ The sandwich is in Steve's _____ .

3. ▶ May is eating a _____ .

4. ▶ You sign your name on a _____
with a pen.

5. ▶ A _____ eats grain and lays eggs.

6. ▶ Mice like to eat _____ .

tch — Catch that pitch!

Tom wa**tch**es his wa**tch**.

scra**tch**

Will can ca**tch** a fast pi**tch**.

ma**tch**   cru**tch**es

Write the word that finishes each sentence.

1. ▶ Will likes to catch, and Steve likes to _____**pitch**_____.

2. ▶ Tom has a _____ that says three o'clock.

3. ▶ May has a _____ on her hand.

4. ▶ Pat lights the fire with a _____.

5. ▶ Will has to walk with _____.

6. ▶ Mike likes to _____ baseball games on TV.

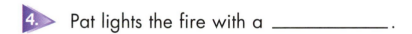

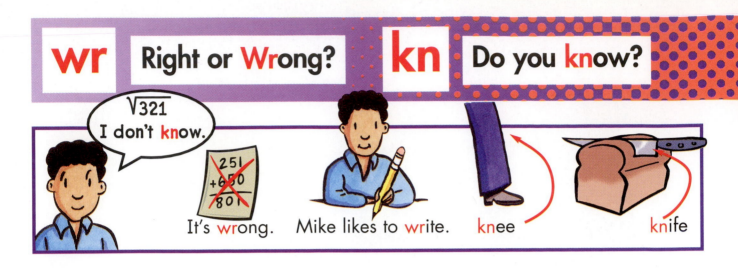

√321
I don't **kn**ow.

251
+650
801

It's **wr**ong.   Mike likes to **wr**ite.   **kn**ee   **kn**ife

Circle *right* if the sentence is correct. Circle *wrong* if it is not correct.

1. ▶ Students write on a desk.   (right)   wrong

2. ▶ Your knee is near your face.   right   wrong

3. ▶ Cats can write.   right   wrong

4. ▶ Math problems make you think.   right   wrong

5. ▶ 229–120=209   right   wrong

6. ▶ Monkeys read and know math.   right   wrong

7. ▶ You can drink milk with a knife.   right   wrong

8. ▶ You can make a sandwich with cheese in it.   right   wrong

9. ▶ A peach is a fruit.   right   wrong

10. ▶ Cats can make a scratch on your hand.   right   wrong

11. ▶ A watch goes on your leg.   right   wrong

12. ▶ You can catch a ball with a mitt.   right   wrong

13. ▶ You can catch a fish with a match.   right   wrong

14. ▶ You can cut a sandwich with a knife.   right   wrong

Going to the Doctor

Scene: A doctor's office. The doctor is checking Will's knee.

Doctor: What is the problem, Will?

Will: I can't walk. I think the problem is in my right knee.

Doctor: Where is the pain? On the top of the knee or on the side?

Will: On the top *and* the side. It feels like a knife is in the knee.

Doctor: Let's see, Will. Can you bend the knee at all?

Will: No. See? It's huge and red.

Doctor: Yes, I see. It is badly swollen. We need to take an X-ray of this knee.

Will: An X-ray? Is it that bad?

Doctor: I don't know for sure, Will. The X-ray is like a photo of the knee. It will show where the problem is.

Will: When can I play baseball again? We have a game on Friday, and I have to catch.

Doctor: Sorry, Will. You may be on crutches this Friday.

Will: Crutches! What bad luck!

Doctor: Let's go take that X-ray. I may be wrong.

Questions

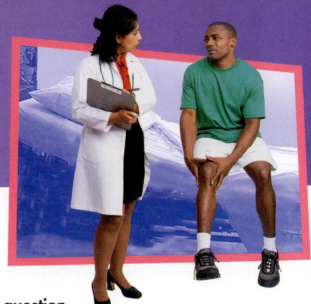

Write a complete sentence to answer each question.

1. ▶ Where is Will? <u>**Will is at the doctor's office.**</u>

2. ▶ What is Will's problem? _____

_____

3. ▶ Where is Will's pain? _____

_____

4. ▶ What does the pain feel like? _____

_____

5. ▶ What is an X-ray? _____

_____

6. ▶ When is Will's baseball game? _____

_____

To discuss:

- Where do you go when you have a pain?
- When do you go to a doctor?
- Is your doctor a man or a woman?
- What can you do to help pain at home?

Words that Rhyme

~~dish~~	scratch	wheat	shine	king	dash
playing	knee	know	that	shake	sheep
glue	walking	write	when	hopping	song
bath	flying	snowing	thinking	these	taking

Write the rhyming word from the box on the line next to each word below.

1. fish _____dish_____

2. then _____

3. cat _____

4. snake _____

5. ring _____

6. long _____

7. line _____

8. math _____

9. meat _____

10. white _____

11. blue _____

12. sleep _____

13. three _____

14. snow _____

15. splash _____

16. catch _____

17. talking _____

18. crying _____

19. stopping _____

20. blowing _____

21. saying _____

22. drinking _____

23. keys _____

24. making _____

Start the car.

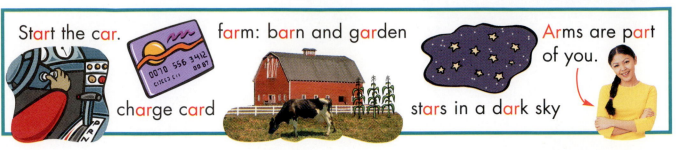

charge card

farm: barn and garden

stars in a dark sky

Arms are part of you.

Write the letter that matches the sentence.

a

b

c

d

e

f

1. ▶ The car has a star on the front. __c__

2. ▶ May's arm is inside the car. ____

3. ▶ You start a car with a key. ____

4. ▶ The sky is dark when it rains. ____

5. ▶ You can shop with a charge card. ____

6. ▶ A barn is part of a farm. ____

er | Summer and Winter Weather

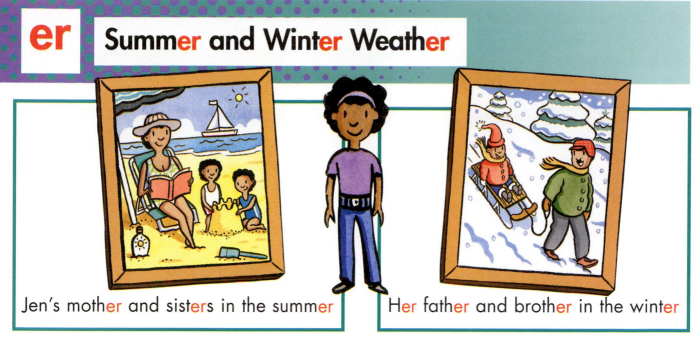

Jen's mother and sisters in the summer | Her father and brother in the winter

Look at the pictures above.
Write the word that finishes each sentence.

1. ▶ Jen's mother and sisters are on the beach in the __**summer**__.
   summer/winter

2. ▶ Her father and _____ are wearing hats in the winter.
   mother/brother

3. ▶ Her brother is riding on a sled in the _____.
   summer/winter

4. ▶ Her _____ is reading a book.
   sister/mother

5. ▶ Her _____ is walking in the snow by the sled.
   father/mother

6. ▶ Her _____ are playing in the sand.
   sisters/brothers

a purple T-shirt

skirt

purse

The girl's sunburn hurts.

nurse

bird

Circle *yes* if the sentence is true. Circle *no* if the sentence is not true.

1.	The T-shirt is purple.	yes	no
2.	A girl can wear a skirt.	yes	no
3.	A bird can hold a purse.	yes	no
4.	A nurse can drive a car.	yes	no
5.	The girl with the blue shirt is Pat.	yes	no
6.	Her sunburn hurts.	yes	no
7.	The nurse has a purple dress.	yes	no
8.	Pat is wearing a skirt on her arms.	yes	no
9.	A charge card can fit in a purse.	yes	no
10.	A bird can drive a car.	yes	no
11.	Girls can play sports.	yes	no
12.	You can get a sunburn in the summer.	yes	no

A Farm in the Valley

Names in the play: Narrator, Pat, her brother, her brother's wife (and baby), her sister, her mother, her father, her grandfather— Joe, and her grandmother

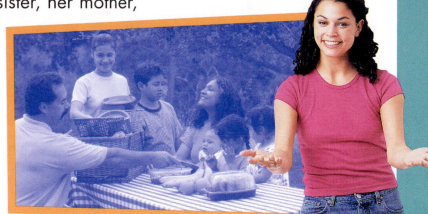

Narrator: Pat's father takes the family in the van to visit Grandpa Joe's farm in the valley. It's summer. The valley is hot, but the farm has many old fruit trees. A table is set under the trees.

Pat: Hi, Grandpa Joe! Grandma, we are here!

Pat's brother: And here is my new baby girl!

Brother's wife: She is just ten weeks old today.

Grandma: Oh, let me see her. What a pretty baby! She has her father's eyes.

Brother: And her mother's smile.

Pat's mother: I am a grandmother, Mama. What do you think of that?

Grandma: I think that means I am a *great* grandmother. What an angel she is.

Grandpa Joe: Come over to the table. It's nice under the trees, and we have lots of ripe peaches for you.

Pat's father: Pat, go help your grandmother with the lunch. Joe and I can watch the baby.

Pat: Okay, but don't let her get a sunburn. Keep her hat on.

Brother's wife: And here is a dry diaper if she gets wet.

Pat's sister: Can Grandpa Joe change a baby?

Grandma: Sure. Joe likes babies as much as fishing.

Pat's father: Is this a good year for the fruit, Joe?

Grandpa Joe: Not bad. We had lots of rain in April and May. Wet weather helps the trees.

Pat's father: Oh, oh. We have a wet baby. Time to go inside.

Questions

Finish the sentences using words from the play.

1. ▶ Pat's father takes the family to visit _____
_____.

2. ▶ The valley is hot, but _____
_____.

3. ▶ Pat's brother and his wife have a _____
_____.

4. ▶ Pat's grandmother says, "Oh, what a pretty baby! She has _____
_____."

5. ▶ Pat says to her father, "Don't let her _____
_____."

6. ▶ Grandma says, "Joe likes _____
_____."

To discuss:

- Do you have a big family?
- Does anyone in your family live on a farm?
- Can a man help a lot with a baby?

over the water

under the water

ten minutes **before** three

ten minutes **after** three

Write the word that finishes each sentence.

1. The star is shining __**over**__ the barn.
  over/under

2. The purse is _____ the car.
  over/under

3. The coat is _____ the purple shirt.
  over/under

4. The key is _____ the mat.
  over/under

5. It is five minutes _____ ten.
  before/after

6. It is fifteen minutes _____ six.
  before/after

7. It is ten minutes _____ eight.
  before/after

8. It is twenty minutes _____ nine.
  before/after

school with a pool and a flat roof

noon

He shoots at the hoop.

food

boots

What are the rules at your school?

Circle *yes* if you can do this at your school. Circle *no* if you can't.
Circle N/A if it does <u>not</u> <u>a</u>pply to you.

1. ▸ Can you chew gum in school?   yes   (no)   N/A

2. ▸ Can you take food into the classroom?   yes   no   N/A

3. ▸ Can you wear boots in school?   yes   no   N/A

4. ▸ Can you wear a baseball cap in school?   yes   no   N/A

5. ▸ Can you take a backpack into the classroom?   yes   no   N/A

6. ▸ Can you wear boots in the gym to shoot hoops?   yes   no   N/A

7. ▸ Can you leave school at noon to eat lunch?   yes   no   N/A

8. ▸ Write a different rule that you have in your school: _____

_____

What do you think is "cool"?

Write an X by the things that you think are "cool."

boots ____   tattoos ____   jeans ____   earrings ____   fast cars ____

Other cool things: _____

_____

ou | **The House**

Write the word that finishes each sentence.

1. ▶ The _____**couch**_____ is in the living room.
   couch/bed

2. ▶ The street sign outside the house says _____ Main St.
   West/South

3. ▶ The mouse is running _____ the house.
   in/around

4. ▶ The bathtub is _____ the house.
   outside/inside

5. ▶ The TV has _____ sounds coming from it.
   soft/loud

6. ▶ The table is in the _____ of the house.
   dining room/kitchen

7. ▶ The dishes are in the _____ in the kitchen.
   sink/bathtub

8. ▶ The cloud is _____ the roof of the house.
   above/below

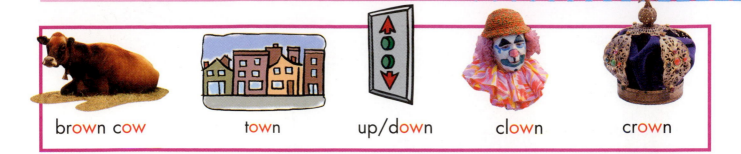

br**ow**n c**ow**   t**ow**n   up/d**ow**n   cl**ow**n   cr**ow**n

Write the word that finishes each sentence.

1. ▶ Cows can be black, white, tan, or __**brown**__.
clown / brown

2. ▶ A king wears a _____ on his head.
crown / cow

3. ▶ Joe lives on a farm, not in a _____.
town / down

4. ▶ The face of the _____ has a big smile.
clown / crown

5. ▶ Rains falls _____ from the clouds.
up / down

6. ▶ _____ many cows are there in the field?
How / Brown

oy | oi   Joyful Noises

joyful party noise   a boy's voice   toy drum   coins   boiling water for tea

Write the word that finishes each sentence.

1. ▶ Singing is the joyful noise a _____**voice**_____ makes.

voice/coin

2. ▶ "Boom" is the loud noise a _____ drum makes.

toy/joy

3. ▶ "Clink" is the noise that _____ make as they drop into a toy bank.

boys/coins

4. ▶ "Yea!" is the noise that _____ and girls yell at a basketball game.

toys/boys

5. ▶ Whistling is the noise a teapot makes when it _____.

boils/coins

What music makes you joyful?

Write an X by the kinds of music that you like.

rap ____   reggae ____   rock ____   blues ____   jazz ____   gospel ____

classical ____   folk ____   salsa ____   country ____   heavy metal ____

Other kinds of music: _____

_____

Going Out

Names in the play: Narrator, Pat, Jen, Tom, Will, May, Mike, Steve, Luz

Narrator: *Jen and Pat are walking out of the high school in the afternoon. Tom, Will, May, Mike, Steve, and Luz are waiting for them near the street.*

Jen: I like your new hoop earrings, Pat. They're cool.

Pat: Thanks. I got them on sale at that new store downtown.

Jen: Hey, there's Will. Are you still going out with him?

Pat: Yes, we're going to the party at Tom's house Friday night. Are you coming?

Jen: I think so. Who else is going?

Pat: The rest of the team and a few guys from out of town.

Will: Jen! Pat! Check this out!

Jen: What do you have?

Tom: I have a new CD for the party.

Pat: [*to Jen*] I know it's going to be a loud rock group. All he likes is hard rock.

Luz: Pat, you will love this. It's salsa!

Pat: Cool! Finally Tom has some music I like.

May: What are you wearing Friday, Luz?

Luz: My new boots.

May: But how can you dance in boots?

Luz: Who is going to dance? I'm just going for the food and the pool.

Mike: Tom has a pool?

Steve: Yes. He lives in a town house with a big pool.

Mike: Do they have a game room, too?

Steve: Sure. And a few basketball hoops outside.

Will: Cool! This is going to be a great party.

Questions

Write a sentence to answer each question.

1. ▶ What is Pat wearing that Jen likes? _____ **Pat is wearing**
   new hoop earrings. _____

2. ▶ What boy is Pat going out with? _____
   _____

3. ▶ What does Tom have for the party? _____
   _____

4. ▶ Where is the party Friday night? _____
   _____

5. ▶ What kind of music do Pat and Luz like? _____
   _____

6. ▶ What does Tom's town house have besides a pool? _____
   _____

To discuss:
- Do you go to parties?
- Do your friends all like the same music?
- Do you like to dance?

cow	school	pool	brown	couch	cloud
hoop	noon	~~food~~	boots	mouse	
voice	bounce	noise	toy	coin	

Write the word from the box that answers the question.

1. ▶ It can be meat or fruit on a plate that you eat for lunch. It is __food__ .

2. ▶ You can swim in it, and it has water in it. It is a _____ .

3. ▶ It means the same as twelve o'clock midday. It is _____ .

4. ▶ It is a little animal that likes to eat cheese. It is a _____ .

5. ▶ You wear them on your feet in the rain. They are _____ .

6. ▶ It is like a long chair that you sit on to watch TV. It is a _____ .

7. ▶ It is the place you go to study and take classes. It is _____ .

8. ▶ You can use it to pay for a bus ride. It is a _____ .

9. ▶ It is a big, black, brown, or tan animal that gives milk. It is a _____ .

10. ▶ A baby or little child likes to play with it. It is a _____ .

11. ▶ It is a lot of loud sounds that you hear in a town. It is _____ .

12. ▶ It is a singing or talking sound. It is a _____ .

13. ▶ It floats high in the sky on a nice day. It is a _____ .

14. ▶ It is round, with a basketball net on it. It is a _____ .

15. ▶ It is a color that is used for shoes and floors. It is _____ .

16. ▶ A ball can do this when it hits the floor. It can _____ .

Word List

a	blue	corn	farm	grain	in
above*	boat	couch	fast	grandma	in back of
after	book*	country*	fat	grandmothe r	in front of
again	boots	cow	father	grandpa	inside
age	bounce*	crab	feel/s	grape/s	is*
all	box*	crown	feet	graph	isn't*
and	boy	crutch/es	fence	grass	it
angel*	bread*	cry/ies	few	gray	it's
animal	brick	cube	field	great*	its
April	bright*	cut	fifteen	green	jacket
are	brother	dance	fifty	ground	jazz
arm	brown	dark	finally	group/s	jeans
around	brush	dash/es	fire	grow/s	Jen
at	Bud	day	fish	gum	jog/s
away	bug	deer	fit/s	guy/s*	joyful
baby	bus	desk	five	gym*	juice*
baby-sit	but	diaper*	flag	hail	jump/s
back	by	different	flakes	happy*	June
backpack	bye	dining room	flat	has*	keep/s
bad	cage*	dish/es	float/s	hat	key
bag	cake	do*	floor	have*	kind/s
ball*	can	doctor	flute	he	king
ballad	can't	dog	fly/ies	head*	kitchen
bananas*	cannot	don't*	folk	heal	knee
barn	cap	door*	food	hear	knife
baseball	car	down	fork	heavy*	know
basketball	cat	downtown	forty	help/s	lake
bat	catch	dress	four*	her	land/s
bath	CD	drink	fourteen	here	last
bathroom	chair	drive/s	fox*	hey*	lay/s
bathtub	change*	drop	Friday	hi	leaf
beach	charge card	drum	frog	hide	leave/s
beans	check	dry/ies	front	high	left
beard	cheese*	ear	fruit	hill*	left hand
bed	chew	earrings	fun	his	leg
bedroom	chicken	earphones	game	hit/s	let
before	class*	easy	garden	hold/s	let's
behind	classroom	eat/s	gas	home plate	life
below	classical	egg	gas pump	home run	light
belt	clear	eight*	get/s	hoop	like/s
bend	clock	eighteen	gift	hop/s	lines
beside/s	clothes*	elephant	girl	hot	little*
Beth	cloud	eleven	give	house	live/s*
between*	clown	else	glad	how	living room
big	coat	eyes*	glass/es	huge*	long
bird	coin	face*	glue	hungry	lot
bite	cold	fall*	go/goes	hurt/s	loud
black	cool	family	goat	I	
blow/s	come/s*	fan belt	gospel	ice*	(continued on next page)

love	noon	race	show/s	swim/s	twenty
low	nose	rain	side	swollen	two*
luck	not	raincoat	sign*	table	umpire
lunch	nothing	rainy	sing/s	tail	under
lunchbox	now	rap	sister	tap	up
Luz	number	read/s	sit/s	tan	use/s
mad	nurse	red	six*	tattoo	valley
mail box	object	reggae	sixteen	team	van
Main	o'clock*	rhyme/s*	sixty	teapots	visit
make/s	of*	ride	skin	tears	voice
man	off*	right	skirt	telephone	wait/s
many*	office	right hand	sky	ten	wake/s up
map	old	ring	sled	tennis*	walk/s*
mat	on	ripe	sleep/s	tent	want*
match	one*	road	slow	test	wash/es
math	open	rock*	smell	that	watch
May	other	roof	smile	the*	water
me	outside	rope	snack	then	waves
meat	over	rose	snail	there*	weather
men	page*	Roth	snake	these	wear/s*
metal	pail	round	snow	they	Wednesday
mice	pain	rowboat	soap	thick	well
midday	pan	rug	socks*	thin	west
Mike	park	rule	soft	think/s	wet
miles	part	run/s	song	thirteen	whale
milk	party/ies	sad	sorry	thirty	what*
minus	past	sale	sound/s	this	wheat
minutes*	Pat	salsa	soup	those	wheel
mitt*	peach	same	south	three	when
Monday	peas	sand	spill/s	throw	whistle*
monkey	pedal/s	sandwich	splash/es	thumb*	white
month/s	pen	say/s	sports	Thursday	wide
mop	phonics	school	stage	time	Will
more	photo	score	stand/s	tire/s	wind (n)
mouse	pick-up truck	scoreboard*	star/s	to*	window
mouth	picnic	scratch	start/s	toe/s	winter
movies	pie	sea	stay	toilet	with
mud	pitch	see/s	step/s	Tom	woman*
music	place	set/s	Steve	tonight	write
my	plane	seven	stick	top	wrong
near	plant	seventeen	still	town	X-ray
need	plate	shake	stop/s	toy/s	years
nest	play	shave/s	store	train	yell/s
net	plus	she	stove	tray	yellow
new	pond	sheep	street	tree	yes
next to	pool	shelf	string	truck	yikes
nice	pot	shine	study	T-shirt	you
night	pretty	ship	summer	tub	your
nine	problem	shirt	sun	Tuesday	yourself
nineteen	purple	shoe/s	sunburn	tune	
no*	purse	shoot/s	sunny	TV	
noise	quiz*	shop/s	sure	twelve	